4 Essential Keys
to
Effective
Communication
in Love, Life, Work—Anywhere!

A **How-To Guide** for Practicing the
Empathic Listening, Speaking, and
Dialogue Skills to Achieve Relationship
Success with the Important People
in Your Life

Including the
**"12-Day
Communication
Challenge!"**

Bento C. Leal III

ISBN: 978-1546581734

Disclaimer: This book is presented to you for informational purposes and is not a substitution for any professional advice. It is the reader's sole responsibility to seek professional advice before taking any action on their part. There are some relationship issues that require more expert intervention than simply reading a book or taking a relationship skills class. Depending on the nature of the issue, it may be more appropriate to seek help from a licensed professional, such as a counselor or therapist. You can also dial 2-1-1 to inquire about services in your area, or visit www.211.org. If you are experiencing a serious issue (such as abuse, domestic violence or other emergency), call 9-1-1 for immediate assistance.

Dear Reader,

As a
Thank You
for getting my book,
I am happy to give
you as a

FREE GIFT

this downloadable and
printable version of the

12-DAY
COMMUNICATION CHALLENGE!
ACTION GUIDE

The Action Guide also appears at the end of
this paperback book, but you might find this
downloadable and printable version even
more convenient for you as you practice
the skills throughout the day.

Go to this link to
download your Free Gift!

www.bentoleal.com/12-day-challenge

Enjoy the Communication Challenge!

Please do me a favor!

Please give me your feedback on
reading my book. Go to Amazon.com,
type in my book title, then scroll down,
and click on
"Write a customer review"
letting me know what you thought
of the book and what you may
have gained from it.

I read each and every review.
They help me a lot.

Thank you!

Praise

"This short book is a jewel, a resource, an important contribution to the growing literature on interpersonal competence. This will be the most useful book you will read this year. Get it, read it, study it, cherish it and use the skills anywhere and everywhere." —**Bill Coffin, Relationship & Marriage Educator; Husband, Father, Grandfather; Marriage Education Specialist (retired), Administration for Children and Families**

"What's the secret of being seen as a great spouse, parent or friend? A great supervisor, employee, teacher, salesperson—any professional? It's listening with empathy, really listening... This little gem of a book reveals the secret of developing this priceless skill. Simple, practical, and effective." —**John R. Williams, Licensed Mental Health Counselor and Marriage & Relationship Educator**

"Bento has written an excellent guide on how to practice empathy in relationships, showing why it's so important and how to do it... This book should be required reading for anyone getting married, since these skills are so essential for a successful marriage." —**Debbie Preece, Marriage Coaching, LLC**

"The communication skills Bento Leal teaches have helped me listen and speak with greater empathy to both my loved ones and my clients, and as a result have continued to strengthen my relationships in my life and work. I highly recommend this book." **—Don Sardella, President, Strategic Consultant & Business Coach, Institute for Leadership Development, LLC**

"This book is a clear and simple guide that can be used to support couples in their communication with each other —and with their children. <u>Every individual can benefit in their work and day-to-day life with better listening and communicating skills by reading and practicing the skills in this book.</u> **—John Abelseth, Family Educator**

Dedication

To my dear wife Kimiko and our children who have shown me the power of love each and every day. Thank you!

Table of Contents

Preface

Welcome to my book. I'm very happy you have it in your hands. I hope you gain a lot from it to enrich your life and relationships.

How to Use this Book

This is very much a **how-to book**—a guide or manual—for learning, practicing, and growing your communication skills and relationships bit by bit, day by day.

To get the most out of the book, read through each chapter with an open mind and a willingness to learn new skills. At the end of most of the chapters is an opportunity for **Self-Reflection** where you are asked a few short questions to contemplate what you just read, consider how it relates to you personally, and determine the appropriate actions to implement the skills in your life.

You can also read and discuss the book as a couple or in a small group or book club, which is a great way to learn and grow together.

BONUS: At the end of the book is the **"12-Day Communication Challenge!"** I encourage you to undertake the challenge as soon as possible after you finish reading the book to jump-start everything you learned in these pages and start growing these skills into your personal habits right away.

With that, let's get started...

Introduction

If you're like most people, you want to have good relationships with the important people in your life—your family, friends, neighbors, co-workers, clients, and customers. At the same time, you have no doubt learned from experience that good relationships don't happen by accident or wishful thinking. They are created, developed over time, and good communication is an essential part of the fabric that creates those relationships.

For more than a decade, I've worked intensively in this fascinating field of interpersonal communication. I've been trained to teach several communication skills curricula and have taught these skills to thousands of individuals and couples, in small groups and large audiences, in churches, social organizations, family resource centers, county jail, federal prison, and other venues.

On every occasion, I'd witness people have profound personal breakthroughs in using these skills to radically improve their communication effectiveness in their marriages, families, at work, and elsewhere.

In this short book, you will learn the *4 Essential Keys to Effective Communication* that I have honed and distilled from my study, teaching, and practice over the past several years. I consider these to be the core fundamentals of successful interpersonal communication.

These skills have helped me greatly in both my personal and professional relationships, and I'm confident these skills will help you achieve relationship success with the important people in your life as well.

Again, I hope you enjoy reading this book and use what you learn to take your relationships to a whole new level of intimacy, satisfaction and success.

All the best,
Bento C. Leal III

Chapter One

How It All Started

It's amazing what you can learn about yourself in a single day.

In April 2005, my wife and I drove up from our home in the Bay Area to attend a relationship skills class in Sacramento, California. I mainly went there on assignment from the president of a non-profit organization I was working with in Oakland. My task was to check out the course to see if it was suitable for teaching low-income clients we were serving in the inner city. So I went there with the idea "I'm going to learn this material to see if it's good for others."

When we got there, I settled into the class with the mindset of being an observer. Within an hour, the instructor started teaching the listening skill, what effective listening consisted of. She asked the class, "Have you had times when you were listening to someone and your mind kept wandering off while they were speaking?" *Yes and often,* I thought to myself. "When a person is speaking to you, do you sometimes think about your response instead of focusing on what they're saying in the moment?" *Hmm, yes again.*

She asked a few more probing questions related to poor or inadequate listening, such as, "Do you sometimes jump in with your own ideas while the speaker is still speaking to you?" and, yes, she was spot on each time.

Almost immediately I felt she was talking directly to me! That was my wakeup call. I realized if what she was saying was what good listening is and can be then I hadn't been listening like that my entire life! It was eye-opening and humbling at the same time.

I'd always thought I was a fairly decent listener—i.e., you speak and I basically understand what you're saying, end of story. But when it came to really *empathizing* with the speaker, and focusing on trying to understand their meaning from *their* point of view, particularly on topics of importance to them, it was clear I was only listening at a surface level much of the time.

I then thought of my wife, my children, and so many others who had been such a major part of my life—I realized that on so many occasions I probably hadn't listened fully and empathically to *any* of them, even though I thought I *was* listening. It was clear that the deeper purpose of my attending this class was for *me* to learn some valuable communication lessons for *myself*, and not simply to learn some good ideas that would benefit others.

That was my introduction into the phenomenal world of empathic communication—what it is, its use, and its powerful impact.

The Importance of Communication Skills in Love, Life, Work—*Anywhere!*

Listening and speaking are the basic communication tools we use every day. We use them to process language as we interact with the people in our lives. When we use these tools well, they help us create wonderful, growing, lasting relationships. However, when used improperly, those very tools of listening and speaking can create a lot of hurt, damage, and even destruction to relationships. The key is to become *skilled* in how to use these essential tools well and put these skills into practice on a daily basis. That's where the real change and growth occurs in oneself and one's relationships.

We have all seen instances, and perhaps experienced ourselves, where a lack of communication skills led to painful consequences—such as a couple speaking hurtfully and disrespectfully to each other over time leading to separation and divorce, or friction between a parent and adult child leading to years of alienation and resentment, or pent up anger and frustration on the job leading to outburst, bad feelings and even termination.

These are all unfortunate consequences of miscommunication. If the parties involved had known and practiced communication skills, these consequences might have been averted.

The good news is there are many excellent communication and relationship skills programs available. Some of the main points and skills they teach are universal and common among them—such as how to listen well, how to express oneself clearly, how to dialogue, manage conflict and problem solve—and the authors of each program have framed and written their version of the skills in their own way with their own unique emphases and exercises. Though they have their unique aspects, all of these programs focus on helping people become better listeners and speakers—core elements of good communication and healthy relationships.

Envision Communication Success

A bit of advice as you read this book: "Begin with the end in mind," as author Stephen Covey would often say. Envision yourself as an effective communicator—the "end" or goal that you want to achieve.

For example, imagine having a conversation with your spouse or partner about your couple's finances, and the conversation is going smoothly. You have different opinions on a few things, but you are discussing them well and without any friction. You are arriving at a budget plan that you both feel very comfortable with.

Then you're at work discussing a project with several co-workers. There are a lot of complicated details being discussed, but you're listening very well to each person's ideas and they feel you understand them. You're also expressing your own ideas to the team thoughtfully and clearly, and the entire conversation is proceeding well, even though there are some conflicting ideas on the team.

Next, you're upset at what your teenage son has done to the family car, but you keep your anger in check and express your frustrations to him clearly but without saying demeaning and hurtful words you'd likely regret later.

In the above scenarios, the communication skills you have learned and practiced are bearing fruit both at home and at work. In your 24/7 world, even in the face of difficulties on several occasions, your relationships are proceeding well. Such results are what we strive for on the road to becoming an effective communicator.

As you start reading this book, envision yourself experiencing relationship success along the way of learning and practicing these solid communication skills. See yourself as that empathic spouse or partner, as an empathic parent, co-worker, neighbor and friend. That vision of yourself as a successful communicator, particularly with the important people in your life, will both drive and pull you ahead.

While the advice and suggestions in this book offer a guide to help you work toward communication success, it's important for you to take ownership of your journey to be the great communicator you want to be. As you do, your compass is set and you can move forward a bit each day toward realizing your goal.

Chapter Two

Empathy—
The Essential Relationship Ingredient

"Could a greater miracle take place than for us to look through each other's eyes for an instant?"
~ Henry David Thoreau

A word that weaves through most relationship skills programs is "empathy", the ability—a developed skill, actually—to vicariously put yourself in another person's shoes and try to see from their point of view, their world, their perspective.

People are more familiar with the word "sympathy", which means to "feel for" someone, particularly if they've experienced a loss of some kind. However, "empathy" means something quite different. The *Oxford Dictionary* defines empathy as "the ability to understand and share the feelings of another." Another way to say it is empathy means to "feel with" or "feel into" as in "feel into the other person", which has powerful impact both for the empathizer and the person being empathized with.

Empathy is a powerful state of mind, but it's not something we try to pound into ourselves, it's something we want to cultivate and *let out*—it's our capacity to have compassion and concern for ourselves and others. Empathy is really an internal motivator to be a caring person who is genuinely concerned about the wellbeing of others, as well as one's own wellbeing.

In this book, I present some of these key communication and relationship skills from my own perspective and experience in their use and value, and they all revolve around this primary skill of empathy.

Chapter Three

An Epiphany

Have you had times when someone was saying something important to you, and they thought you were listening but you really weren't? Your mind had wandered off and you couldn't recall what they said? Maybe you were tired or had other things on your mind or it just wasn't the right moment for you to give your full attention? If you answered yes, you're not alone. This is a common communication challenge.

About four years ago, I had an epiphany in dealing with this very issue. I was listening to a friend tell me about a new project at his work he was excited about. I tried to slide into the sincere listening mode, which I had been trained in and taught others, of focusing on what he was saying and his underlying feelings about it, but my mind kept wandering off to some things I needed to do. I'd catch myself going off track and then try to refocus on him and what he was saying.

Now, this wasn't the first time this lack of attentiveness had happened to me—in fact, this would often happen in my conversations with people. But for some reason, in this particular conversation my lack of attentiveness to what he was saying struck a deep chord in me. While he was talking, and during this back and forth of focusing, drifting and refocusing, I caught and asked myself, *Wait a minute, do I really* care *about what he's*

---

saying? I had to honestly say to myself, *Maybe not*—at least not in that moment.

Then I said to myself, *He's really excited about what he's talking about. Can't I give him a few undistracted minutes of my time and simply listen?* At that moment, the answer was yes, I could. *But do I care, do I really want to?* This thought led to another track, *How much do I really care about a person—especially someone I know well—if I have to wrestle in my mind to give him (or her) a few minutes of my undivided attention, especially when he's telling me something of importance to him?*

Part of my problem in the moment was that I not only didn't value what he was saying, but I wasn't showing him that I valued him enough as a person to give him the full attention he deserved. In the very moment I was focusing on doing communication "skills" with him, I had forgotten about the overall *purpose* of communication, which is to make a connection with him, to understand what he was saying and meaning, particularly because it was a topic of importance to him.

This thought of not valuing him enough as a person brought me back to considering what I'd learned since I was a child—that each person is a special being, unique in all the universe, a person of immense and unique value worthy to be loved and respected. *That's great philosophy,* I thought, *but what about in real life?* Surely, if I considered people to be special and unique beings then what they were saying would have greater meaning to me and I'd be able to focus on what they were saying more deeply, more sincerely, more empathically, and they'd sense it as well.

This flipped a switch in me—I needed to practice *seeing* each person as a special and unique individual, whether I knew them well or not. The communication *skills* of listening and speaking I had been focusing on were the tools, the *how*, but it was often very easy for me to lose touch with the overall *why*—making a deeper emotional connection with this valuable other human being.

(**NOTE:** It's important to clarify here that much of the communication in our daily lives consists of simply the conveying of facts or some ordinary bits of information that are expressed and responded to without much emotional significance, such as, "Honey, I'm going to the store," or, "Did you return that call to Joe?" However, as will be discussed in greater detail later, when deeper emotions are being conveyed, such as your partner saying with a sigh, "Whew, I really had a difficult time at work today," or, "I'm starting to get worried about our financial situation," that's when empathy and emotional alertness are needed to make a more internal connection between the speaker and the listener.)

Looking in the Mirror

Then I turned the mirror on myself. If this friend of mine and every other person are unique and valuable individuals, then so am *I*, and I needed to see myself in that way as a person of immense, unique value. Not just once in a while but often. Actually, always!

Let me pose the same question to you: If you were to look in the mirror, who would you see? Yourself. And just by being yourself, wouldn't that be enough to know that you are also unique? If you were to take a second to think about yourself—and *really* think about yourself—my hope is that you'd likewise see that you are valuable. Your thoughts. What makes you happy. Those whom you love and care about. All those things that make you who you are. And it's those things that truly make you special. And with that logic, if you're valuable and special, then the people who surround you are also valuable and special. But in reality, with everything going on in our lives, how often do we take the time to actually stop and think about our value and the value of those we love? Perhaps not often enough.

I knew that even though this was a good wake-up call for me—a reminder that we are each a unique, special, valuable human being—this perspective wouldn't be my automatic default frame of mind from then on simply because I had an "aha" moment. It would be a *skill* I would need to develop and mindfully practice just like any other skill I had learned, such as swimming, typing, or driving a car.

But it's not that easy to change a habit from behaving a certain way, especially a habit a lifetime in the making. It's a challenge to see myself and others with that fresh, positive, value-identifying perspective. To see the good rather than the bad. To look from a higher viewpoint and see the special and unique rather than the normal and mundane. It would be a skill I would have to break up into bite-sized steps and practice, but in the end would be well worth the effort to achieve.

I decided to call this skill of mindfully valuing oneself and others *Empathic Awareness Skill* because it involves each of those words:

1) *Empathy* – putting yourself in the other person's shoes, their point of view, their perspective, trying to feel what they're feeling

2) Being mindfully *Aware* that each person has unique, special value

3) It's a *Skill*, a learned and practiced behavior—something that is developed over time

Here are the skill steps…

Chapter Four

Key 1: Empathic Awareness Skill

Each person is unique, special, valuable.

Empathic Awareness Skill is something we do before we even start to communicate with someone and while we communicate with them. It's our internal perspective, our frame of mind, the lens, the heart through which we see ourselves and others. It's the *why* we communicate, and that is the reason I consider it to be the foundational skill for all the other skills.

Empathic Awareness Skill has 4 steps:

Step 1: Recognize your own inherent value and dignity as a person. Your inner self. Your unique value and special character. See the best in you!

It's vital to cultivate a self-awareness of our own personal value, such that we can honestly think to ourselves (and even say aloud), "I am unique, special, and valuable." Truly, there is no one else like you or me in all the world. We are each one of a kind with our own unique talents, abilities and personality.

"Put your own mask on first"

If we don't believe in *our own* value, how will we believe in the value of *others*? When you're on an airplane, the flight attendant tells everyone that if there is a loss in cabin air pressure the oxygen mask will drop from overhead and to put yours on first before you try to help someone else; otherwise, you won't be able to breathe and you won't be much help to anyone. Similarly, if we aren't able to recognize our own value first, it will be more difficult to turn and see the value of others.

In fact, the most common teaching in the world's religions is a form of "love others as you love yourself" and even self-help professionals express forms of this teaching. However, it only works if a person loves and values him or herself. People who don't love or value themselves can actually be harmful, both to themselves and to others, because if they don't appreciate themselves then they very likely will not appreciate others.

Ways to enhance Empathic Awareness of our personal value and potential:

- **Meditation, Self-Reflection, Prayer:**
  These are time-honored practices to help calm the mind and body, eliminate distractions, clear the mental and spiritual air, and connect with the deeper, positive mind within oneself—our internal essence. If you're a religious or spiritual person, this is pausing to connect to a higher power, your life source.

- **Inspirational and Motivational Books:**
  These words have the power to instruct, uplift and energize your thinking and bolster your sense of self and self-value. These words are food for the mind and soul. Inspirational and motivational books can help you recognize your value as well as identify and nurture your unique talents and potential.

- **Speeches, Seminars, Webinars, Workshops, Sermons:**
  The more exposure we have to uplifting, thought-provoking information and testimonies from others that give us greater understanding and awareness of our own value, talents, and capacities the more we should take them and invest in them—we'll be the better for it.

- **Positive Self-Talk:**
  We are what we think. Fill your mind with positive self-talk (*I can do it, I'm a person of great value, I have talents that can help others*). Think positive thoughts and expectations about yourself and others, your goals, relationships, and life in general and those things are more likely to come to fruition. Norman Vincent Peale, author of the classic *The Power of Positive Thinking,* may have said it best: "Change your thoughts and you change your world."

  On the contrary, if you fill your mind with nega-tive self-talk (*I can't, I'm no good, There's no way*) then *those* things will likely come true. In a very real sense we reap what we sow in our minds—positive thoughts produce positive words, actions and results; negative thoughts produce negative words, actions and results. How we direct our thinking, self-talk, and attitude determines which way we go.

Step 2: Recognize the inherent value and dignity of the other person, that they are likewise worthy of respect.

As mentioned above, every human being is special, regardless of their level of income, social status or other characteristic. We are fellow travelers on this planet, in this time and space. Of all the people who are alive now, and who have ever lived or will live, the people we encounter each day are in our very presence, our sphere of awareness. We can even think there is some purpose for their being in our world—something we can learn from them, and something they can learn from us.

Each person has their strong points and weak points, faults and quirks, but also, like us, they are unique, special, valuable—we need to see them that way, treat them that way. I suggest that this is a prerequisite to being able to have good communication, in that we are grateful for these people in our lives and can acknowledge that every single person may have something to teach us and help us grow. In fact, you might notice something special in them they don't even see in themselves.

Pause → Reflect → Adjust → Act

I've found this to be a very helpful mantra: *Pause. Reflect. Adjust. Act.* It's like an inner compass helping to steer myself in the right direction. Often, in the course of the day, while I'm communicating with someone and my mind starts to drift or my sense of being empathic starts to fade, I'll catch myself and think, *Pause. Reflect. Adjust. Act.*

The *Pause* helps me stop my wayward thinking on the spot—like a stoplight. Then I *Reflect* on the importance of the person and what they're talking about or the situation, I *Adjust* my focus and intentionality to value and zero in on them and what they're saying and feeling, and finally I *Act* by being more empathically present.

This mantra and state of mind act as a realignment tool. Like driving a car or flying a plane, we are constantly making adjustments to stay on the path toward our destination. In this case, that destination is being empathically aware of ourselves and the other person in the moment.

"But what about a person I don't like?"

Let's face it, there are many people we may not like for one reason or another—their attitude, personality, behavior, the way they talk or dress, their breath!—but even regarding them, you can look at the bright side and think, *This difficult person may be in my life so that I can: 1) grow my heart to unconditionally value him/her and 2) look in the mirror to see if I need to change something about myself, such as overcome my anger, impatience, or some other negative behavior trait I have. I can learn something valuable from them, and they can learn something valuable from me.*

Think of the people in your life that you don't particularly like—that nosy acquaintance, the relative who talks too much, your untidy neighbor, an arrogant co-worker. As much as you dislike some of their behaviors and attitudes, try looking beyond those characteristics and think, *They may be a test for me to grow my heart of empathy and compassion for who they are as unique human beings.*

You can also think, *Perhaps they agitate something in me that I need to confront and deal with—my own arrogant and judgmental attitudes, my hair-trigger anger, my prejudice, etc.* Indeed, these people who are challenging for you to deal with may be an opportunity to stretch your heart and grow your character. Who knows, you may be challenging to them!

Act Loving in order to *Feel* Loving

Dr. Jerome Bruner, Harvard psychologist, writes, "You are more likely to *act* yourself into feeling than *feel* yourself into action." The lesson here is to *act* loving in order to *feel* loving rather than simply wait for loving feelings to emerge before you act. If we act loving and caring even to someone we don't like, the feelings of love and caring will sooner or later emerge within us. Thus, we *acted* ourselves *into the feelings* we wanted to have.

The **Golden Rule** says, "Do unto others as *you* would have them do unto *you*." But there's also a **Platinum Rule** which I believe is even more explicitly other-centered: "Do unto others as *they* would have you do unto *them*." That's empathy or compassion—seeing and feeling the other person from *their* point of view, putting yourself in *their* shoes, *their* frame of reference.

Ways we can enhance our Empathic Awareness of others:

- Think of this day as an **experiment** in which you see the people you come in contact with as opportunities for you to grow in love and compassion by practicing caring, understanding, patience, forgiveness and gratitude. Test the hypothesis that Empathic Awareness will work in your life today.

- Take the **1-Day Empathy Challenge!** Practice seeing the people you meet today as a *gift*—a unique opportunity to grow your heart and empathy.

Step 3: **Create the <u>desire</u> in your mind to <u>want</u> to listen and relate to them**—to feel and understand them as they are.

Intentions precede actions. As we create the *desire*—the intention—to relate well with others because we recognize their value as unique and special human beings, that desire will fuel and mobilize our *want* to listen and relate to them and move us closer to doing so. We're moving from internal realization of its importance to the external action of doing it. Cultivating such intentionality within our heart and mind is a deliberate act on our part, an act of focus and sincerity, and a vital element of the *Empathic Awareness Skill.*

In his book *Real Love*, Dr. Greg Baer says, "Real Love is caring about the happiness of another person without any thought for what we might get for ourselves." Cultivating such love in our hearts moves us toward loving actions, and the more we uplift the other person the more we are uplifted in the process. The smile on their face brings a smile to our own.

Author Josephine Billings similarly said, "To the world you may be one person, but to one person you may be the world." The love we give another person may be the very thing that gives them hope—helps them feel their value.

We need to reach out with our eyes, ears, words, and attitude to make a connection of heart with that person. An unexpected benefit of *Empathic Awareness* is that in reaching to understand and relate to the deeper heart and feelings of another person this will take us deeper into our own heart, similar to getting to the same water level. Simply put, we can't get to a deeper place in someone else from a shallow place in ourselves.

Step 4: **Think of the <u>positives</u> in your relationship with the other person**—your spouse, child, parent, friend, co-worker, etc. Even a stranger—they're in your world too!

Thinking of the positives about other people and our relationship to them creates an attraction, a magnetic effect drawing us toward them. We're focusing on the positives, what's bright about them, rather than focusing on repelling any negatives. Our positive perspective is the key and a powerful aspect of *Empathic Awareness Skill.*

Ways to develop our positive perspective of others:

- **Focus on the good.** Think of the qualities and characteristics we appreciate about them—for example, the co-worker trying their best on that particular project even though they may not always clean up after themselves in the lunchroom; our spouse or partner constantly giving us encouraging words even though they are sometimes late for appointments; the neighbor working two jobs to support his family even though their front yard looks kind of shabby. When we focus on the positives of who they are and what they do, it will help us put any negatives into better perspective, even if we need to discuss and problem-solve some of those negatives with them. Our positive attitude opens up our heart to the possibilities of what can go right instead of what can go wrong.

- **The Eye of the Beholder**. What we look for we will find. If we look for good qualities in another person, we will find them. On the other hand, if we expect and look for the bad or imperfect qualities, we will find those as well. It really depends on our point of view, our lens, our expectation, our intention. Think of it as putting on "empathy glasses"—seeing the best in the other person, seeing them and their needs from their point of view.

Is Empathic Awareness Realistic?

Now you might say, "This all sounds very nice, but is being empathically aware doable or even practical in the course of our busy lives? Is achieving that state of mindfulness on a day-to-day basis realistic?" It's definitely a challenge. At the same time, the goal of becoming an empathic person is to become a better person. Even if it's small changes like taking the time to listen better or intentionally pausing to understand what the other person is really feeling, it's often these little things that can make a big difference.

Think of It as a Skill

If you think of achieving greater *Empathic Awareness* of the value of yourself and others as a "skill" that you learn and cultivate in yourself and get better at over time with practice then it may appear more doable to you. We all know from experience that becoming skilled at anything doesn't happen by chance or accident or by wishful thinking. It requires learning what to do and steady intentional effort, practicing it with successes and failures along the way as we get better and better at it.

For example, I wanted to learn how to play the guitar when I was a teenager so that I could play some of the popular songs of the day as well as write my own. I bought a guitar and a chord book and started to figure it out, but it took several weeks of trial and error and lots and lots of practice before my fingers finally did what I wanted them to do. Many times it was frustrating, but I kept at it. Now, decades later, it's automatic—when I want to play a C chord, my fingers jump immediately to the exact position on the strings and I strum the C chord. I wanted the skill, I learned and practiced it, and now it's an ingrained behavior, a part of me.

In recent years, I wanted to become more intentional in my communication skills with other people and have a greater *Empathic Awareness* of each person's unique value as I'm communicating with them. As with playing the guitar, the same learning and practice of skills apply, and I've noticed that my focus and practice of communication skills is paying off bit by bit, day by day. I must admit I still have a long way to go, but I'm making progress.

Opportunities for Growth Every Day!

The good news is that opportunities for developing your *Empathic Awareness Skill* show up all the time, even daily and unexpectedly. You're driving on the freeway, and a driver cuts you off and you want to get angry at him. A co-worker won't stop complaining and you're getting fed up with him or her. We may not know what personal issues they may be dealing with or be able to control or modify their behavior, but we can control and modify our own.

We can think of those situations as opportunities to remind ourselves about the importance of *Empathic Awareness Skill* and to try to practice it. Use empathy as the foundation for understanding. Recognize that the intent behind the other person's behavior may not be to upset or antagonize you. Instead, take that understanding and own the situation. Again, while we can't control the world around us, we can control our reactions to it.

These words by writer Robin Sharma are encouraging. "What you focus on grows, what you think about expands." Striving to master the skill of *Empathic*

Awareness of the value of yourself and others is a very worthy life goal. As we focus on it, it will expand.

Without the underlying perspective of valuing the other person, the communication skills of listening and speaking would be merely information exchange techniques—but what would actually be running *through* that exchange? Information only? The answer should be a heart to value and appreciate another human being. For when it's all said and done, most would agree that one of the highest values of life is having good relationships.

Summary:

Empathic Awareness of the value and dignity of myself and others is the starting point for good communication to take place.

The 4 Steps of Empathic Awareness Skill:
1) Recognize your own inherent value and dignity as a person.
2) Recognize the inherent value and dignity of the other person, that they are likewise worthy of respect.
3) Create the desire in your mind to want to listen and relate to them.
4) Think of the positives in your relationship with the other person.

Self-Reflection:

1) As I reflect on the above, how would I honestly rate my *Empathic Awareness* of the unique and special value and dignity of *(√ below)*:

	Low 1	2	3	4	High 5
Myself					
People close to me (family, friends, etc.)					
People at work (co-workers, customers, etc.)					
People in general					

2) Is *Empathic Awareness Skill* something I want/need to be more conscious of and better at?

> Yes ___ No ___ Somewhat ___ Not Sure ___

3) If yes or somewhat, what aspects of *Empathic Awareness Skill* do I want to improve and grow?

_____

_____

_____

_____

4) What **actions** will I take to improve or grow my *Empathic Awareness Skill,* and with whom?

_____

_____

_____

_____

Now let's look at how well we listen to others when they are speaking to us...

Chapter Five

Key 2: Empathic Listening Skill

"Most people do not listen with the intent to understand; they listen with the intent to reply."
~ Stephen R. Covey

The Question: "How can I listen in a way that I accurately understand the other person, such that they feel truly heard and understood by me, especially on an emotional topic?"

In every class I've ever taught, and I've taught many and continue to, it's the Listening Skill where the greatest "aha" moments happen for the class participants. Most come to the same realization that I did—that their listening skills have not been very good and can be greatly improved.

As I mentioned earlier, I was trained and certified to teach several communication skills courses. Each course focuses on listening skills in one way or another. It's called by many names—reflective listening, active listening, power listening, etc. In any case, they each highlight the importance of being empathic to the speaker, quieting your own mind and putting yourself in their shoes so that you accurately understand them and they feel understood.

Common Couple Complaint

One of the most common complaints among couples in the field of relationship enrichment is, "He doesn't listen to me," and, "She doesn't listen to me." In fact, they're probably *both* right, and, not surprisingly, this can create a wall of separation between them that gets thicker over time. They routinely misunderstand each other, leading to feelings of hurt and frustration, and one or both of them either give up and stop trying or break off the relationship altogether.

But what I've seen in many cases, when they learn and practice the listening skills, is that they each come to the conclusion that their partner *was* right, that they *hadn't* been listening as well as they could, and that *they each* need to become better listeners.

As one woman admitted during a class, "I thought it was *his* problem of not listening to me, and that's why I was so frustrated. But I realized that I hadn't been listening well to him either. A lot of the problem was *me*."

In the instances when couples, or even one of the partners, come to that realization, the door is then open for them to put that realization into practice by making changes in behavior that can grow and, in some cases, even save their relationship.

Back from the Brink

I remember one instance at the end of a communication skills class when this young lady, with her husband sitting next to her, stood up and appreciated the course and getting to know everyone and said, "You all didn't know this, but before we came to this class my husband and I decided we had had enough of each other and were going to file for a divorce." This surprised everyone. She continued, "We have three small children, but we felt we just couldn't take it anymore. But after attending this class, and especially learning the listening skills, we both realized we had been poor listeners and misunderstood each other a lot, which just made things worse and worse. We now have a skill that will help us listen better. We have hope now to make a new start together as a couple and family."

This is the power of *Empathic Listening*—it can help make a healthy relationship even better, and it can help a relationship that's veered off course move back into a positive direction.

Empathic Listening Skill has 5 steps:

Step 1: Quiet your mind and focus on the other person as they are speaking. Put yourself in their world, look from their point of view.

This means not only being silent and not speaking when the other person is talking but also quieting your mind from distracting thoughts that prevent you from really listening. I've certainly found this to be a challenge myself, and I assume you have also. When the other person is speaking, it's easy to mentally drift away or think,

When will they get to the point? or, *I wonder what's for lunch*, or glance at the clock on the wall to get the time, etc.

These distractions take us away from being fully present in the here and now and receptive to what the speaker is saying. It takes conscious awareness, self-discipline, and practice to focus correctly and consistently on the other person while they're speaking. We need to remind ourselves throughout the day of its importance and make the effort. As we listen to what the other person is saying, focusing on their underlying feelings about what they're saying, and try to get "locked in" to their perspective, the peripheral distractions will start to disappear.

Step 2: **Listen <u>fully</u> and <u>openly</u> to what they are saying**, in their words and body language, without bias, defensiveness or thinking about what you'll say next. *Actively* listen.

Interpersonal communication has been the subject of several research studies over the years. Perhaps not surprisingly, they have concluded that the majority of interpersonal communication is non-verbal, meaning communication is not simply the processing of words. What the research found is that body language, facial expression, tone of voice, posture, eye contact or lack of it *say* a lot.

For example, if someone is saying, "You're great," or, "That was a really smart thing to do," but they roll their eyes sarcastically, what are they *really* saying? Something other than what was implied by their words alone. Thus, we might listen more through our *eyes* than through our *ears*! All the more reason to listen intently to what the other person is saying and conveying to us. As we do so, we'll more likely get the full meaning of what they're communicating.

Also, listening without bias or defensiveness or thinking what we'll say next really comes into play when we may be having a conversation involving high emotions, differences of opinion or an argument. In those cases, it's easy to slip into preparing our response or rebuttal rather than listening clearly and fully to what the other person is saying.

Here's the Problem

If, for example, you're talking to me about something I disagree with you on, and I'm simply thinking about my response or rebuttal to what you're saying and not fully listening to you, then I might respond to something you didn't really say or intend because I wasn't listening!

I've seen this problem with many couples in my classes. Because they didn't listen fully to each other, they often misunderstood what the other was saying and implying, which led to even greater misunderstandings and feelings of hurt, anger, and even resentment—all because they weren't fully listening to each other in the first place.

Oftentimes correcting this one thing enabled the couples to communicate much more easily with each other and discuss and work through topics of disagreement much more successfully. Issues that had been hang ups and huge problems for them were often dealt with and resolved simply by slowing down the process to hear each other fully.

Step 3: **Listen "through the words"** to the deeper thoughts and feelings that you sense from the speaker.

Keep in mind that emotions are feelings—they are not in word form. When someone wants to express in words what they are feeling (their wants, desires, concerns, etc.) they take those feelings and cycle them through their brain to try to come up with the best words (vocabulary) to explain those feelings in a coherent way. The words they choose and the sentences they say are the best they can come up with in the moment. If you listen only to the words then you might miss a lot of the underlying meaning.

Only a small percentage of an iceberg is above the water line. Most of it is underneath and unseen. Likewise, if I listen only to the words you say, and with only *my* definition of those words, then I might get only a surface understanding of what you're trying to communicate. But if I try to listen *through* the words to grasp your underlying meaning and intent of the words, I have a greater chance of getting to and understanding your deeper thoughts and feelings.

For example, if you tell me you just lost your job but that you're confident you'll get another one soon and I only listen to your words, I might conclude that you've only hit a minor bump in the road and you're not too bothered by it. But if I see the worry on your face and hear your wavering tone of voice and listen through the words to the reality that you just lost your primary source of income, that all adds up to me that you're far more concerned about your situation than your surface words of confidence alone would seem to indicate.

All She Needed Was for Me to Listen

A few years back, my daughter was working on her thesis for graduate school and when we'd meet for lunch or a chat, she would say that it was going "Okay". But on this one occasion, I saw her biting her lip (something she would do when she was nervous) and look to the side and not in my eyes when she was talking. I knew that writing her thesis and all the research was stressful, but at that moment I realized that it was much more stressful and emotionally taxing than I had initially thought. Maybe it wasn't "okay" after all.

The conversation easily could have moved on from there, but I could see that there may be more to the story. I asked her about her advisor and she said, "She didn't really like some of my ideas, so I need to go back and research more ... again." She let out a sigh and her shoulders started to hunch. Now, an option for me to respond would have been, "Well, that's great that you can go and keep moving with another idea."

But that wasn't really the point here. As I kept listening "through her words", it was clear that she felt defeated and was losing confidence in her ability to write a successful thesis. I didn't give any advice, I just listened. And after I took the time to listen to her and support her, I could tell she felt more relieved. She felt more comfortable to open up about her frustrations and was able to use me as a sounding board to talk through her challenges and come up with her own solutions.

Ultimately, with her new sense of confidence, she did go back and continued to research, developed her argument further, got approval from her advisor, produced a wonderful thesis, and got her master's degree. But the point of the story is, in the moment when she was feeling down, I was able to listen to her with empathy, and that's what she needed at that time.

Listening is really a very *active* act. It's not simply where you throw the words (active) and I catch the words (passive). Rather, it's you throw the words (active) and I *reach out* with my mind and senses to *catch the essence* of what you're saying and implying (active). Thus, sincere *Empathic Listening* is really an adventure—it's reaching out and into, striving to understand the depth of what the speaker is communicating from *their* point of view.

Step 4: Don't interrupt them as they are speaking to you or try to finish their sentences. *Just listen!*

Interrupting other people when they are speaking is a major communication problem. Almost everyone I've known and those I've taught in my classes admit that they sometimes (or often) do this—they think they are showing empathy by 'engaging' the speaker by talking while the speaker is talking or they think this will help speed up the conversation.

In one of my women's classes in federal prison, I had the women pair up to have a practice conversation about a person they admire and why. My instruction was that they would choose who would go first, and that person would speak and their partner would listen intently without interrupting them.

After a few minutes of the first person speaking, I asked the pairs to switch roles so that the speaker became the listener, and the listener became the speaker. After several minutes of doing this, I brought the class back together and asked, "What was that like?" One of the ladies said, "It was so difficult for me not to butt in to what she was saying. I'd always thought if we're not both talking at the same time, the other person would think I'm not engaged in the conversation." I asked her partner what it felt like to be listened to without interruption. She smiled and said, "We've been friends for quite a while, and this is the first time I felt she heard everything I wanted to say." They both chuckled, but the message was clear. She finally felt listened to and understood. This was an important lesson for everyone—the power of *Empathic Listening*.

"Well, let me get there!"

On another occasion, I'll never forget what a pastor's wife said in a small class I taught a few years ago. It was a class of six pastor couples who had gotten together at a church for communication skills training.

I had just taught them the listening skill when one of the wives turned to her husband (senior pastor of their church) and said, "I'm tired of talking to you!" He looked at her stunned, and the rest of us were stunned too. He asked, "Why?" and she said, "Every time I try to tell you something, you go and try to finish my sentence!" "Well, I think I know where you're going to go with that," he said, to which she replied, "Well, let me get there!"

Let the speaker finish what they're saying—don't jump in and try to finish their sentence even if you think it's helpful; it will only cut them off and make it your statement instead of theirs. They've got the floor, let them get to their own finish line. They will appreciate it, and greater understanding will result from it.

Step 5: **Say back to them, in your own words, what they said and their feelings that you sensed from them** to make sure you understand them correctly and they feel understood.

This is a powerful aspect of *Empathic Listening*. When you say back to the speaker the essence of what you heard them say, this accomplishes two things: 1) it helps confirm that you heard what they said and meant—that you got it correctly and you understand them, and 2) it helps the speaker know what they sounded like, what they communicated. They may think they explained themselves fully, but by your feedback—saying back in your own words what they said—they will clearly know if it was enough or if they need to explain more.

Assurance You Were Listening

Also, when the speaker hears their own content coming back to them from the listener, it gives them assurance that you were really listening, that you cared enough to make sure you understood them correctly. That's very reinforcing and validating to the speaker— that what they said was important enough to be heard and that you took them seriously enough to get it right.

This also avoids pitfalls of misunderstanding. For example, if you tell me something important and I only nod my head, you might get the impression that I understood everything you wanted to communicate. But how would you know just by my head nod? Who knows, I might be nodding at an incorrect understanding of what you said. To avoid this error, my saying back the main points of what I heard you say and the feelings I sensed from you makes it clear whether I got it right or not, and if I didn't get it right, then you can correct me. So my saying back the essence of what you said helps us be on the same page of what you were trying to communicate to me.

Examples of saying back in your own words what the speaker said:

Example 1:
Speaker with a down expression on her face and in her voice: "Our dog died yesterday. We had her for 15 years. She was a wonderful dog, a member of our family."

- **Listener** with a similar somber tone and facial expression: "You really miss her."
- **Speaker:** "Yeah, she was the best."
- **Result:** The speaker feels you sense their pain.

Example 2:
Speaker with enthusiasm: "We had the best time ever in the mountains—clear blue skies, beautiful scenery, fresh air—I loved it!"

- **Listener** smiling: "Wow, sounds like you had an absolutely wonderful time!"
- **Speaker:** "We sure did!"
- **Result:** The speaker feels you're resonating with their joy.

Example 3:

Speaker appearing frustrated: "My job is really rough right now—so many tasks to do and so little time to get them done."

- **Listener** with a look of concern: "You feel totally overwhelmed with all you have to do."
- **Speaker:** "Yeah, I feel swamped."
- **Result:** The speaker feels you understand how overburdened and stressed out they are.

As the listener, notice that your responses simply indicate that you empathically heard and felt what the speaker was communicating. You're not fixing anything, providing a solution or even trying to encourage and reassure them—you're simply listening with empathy and connecting with *their* thoughts and emotions. In that moment, the speaker feels, "Someone understands me," and that's the point. Your suggestions, reassurance, etc., can be expressed after—but first it's important to connect with their emotion and their feelings, that's the key of empathy.

Your Good Listening Can Help the Speaker

Oftentimes, just by you being a good listener the speaker can express their thoughts and feelings, sort out what's on their mind, and even come to their own resolutions about what they need to do, and all you did was listen. As noted American psychologist Carl Rogers once said, "We think we listen, but very rarely do we listen with real understanding, true empathy. Yet listening, of this very special kind, is one of the most potent forces for change that I know."

When there are so many emotions swirling inside a person, they have the need to express those feelings in words in order for them to actually hear and understand more clearly what's going on inside their own mind and heart. They may need to talk it out so that they can see all the pieces and how they fit together before their emotions make sense to them. In that case, if you're the listener, it's helpful to simply listen. You don't need to offer advice or say what you would do in their situation, etc.—just listen. Your good listening provides a sounding board for them to hear what they're thinking and helps them become clearer in their own mind.

"Why won't they talk to me?"

Sometimes a spouse, partner, parent or co-worker might wonder in frustration about a person close to them who they wish would express themselves more and share their feelings with them. "Why won't they talk to me? Why don't they tell me what's on their mind, what they're concerned about? Why are they so quiet?" There may be several reasons and one might be that they're not sure it's safe to say what they want to say without being misunderstood, ridiculed, or deluged with a lot of unsolicited advice or suggestions. If they've experienced some of those things in the past, they are liable to clam up, be silent, and keep their thoughts to themselves. In their mind, it's better to be safe than sorry.

If you want a person to open up and share more of what's on their mind, make it safe and comfortable for them to do so by simply being a good listener.

Apology as Door-Opener

One possible reason the person may be quiet and not talking is that they may be harboring a hurt or resentment about something you may have said or done recently or in the past. You want them to open up, but they are reluctant to do so. A sincere apology may be the key to unlock the door.

A woman in one of my classes had a hard time getting her teenage son to open up to her about what was going on in his life and the challenges he was having. She would say to him, "Why won't you talk to me? I want to know what's going on with you. I want to be helpful." But he wouldn't budge. She was frustrated and even getting angry about it.

But one evening as she sat and pondered the situation, she reflected on some of the things she had been learning in the class. She then considered his perspective by putting herself in his shoes. She realized her own behavior may have caused his silence. *I need to say something,* she thought to herself. She approached him and said, "I've been learning some communication skills in a class I'm taking, and I've come to realize that the way I communicated was very poor on many occasions." She continued, "I want you to know that I love you. You mean the world to me. If I've said or done some things in the past that hurt you, I'm sorry." Her son listened, sensed her sincerity, and started to share some instances where he felt put down, misunderstood, scolded for no reason, etc., and she listened. He vented a lot. She didn't push back, react, or offer excuses, she simply listened.

Ultimately, he needed to get those things off his chest, and she needed to hear it. Her apology triggered the opportunity, and he felt listened to and understood. After that experience, the clouds in their relationship began to disappear. They are communicating more and better now, and their relationship is on the upswing.

If a person you want to communicate with is non-responsive to or even rejecting your attempts at conversation, review in your mind if there were any recent occasions where you may have hurt their feelings or caused them distress in some way. If so, that may be a major reason, if not the reason, for their reluctance to communicate. You may need to express an apology. An apology can often work wonders to clear the air and enable honest, candid communication to flow and relationships to renew.

The Fixer

Here's another issue that often comes up in communication. In many relationships, one of the partners tends to be the one who handles many of the physical tasks that require tools and know-how; in other words, they're "the fixer".

Some people tend to be "trained fixers"—they expect to be the go-to persons to get those physical tasks done. I'm a trained fixer. If my wife says, "Honey, the light is off in the hallway," I know that's my cue to go and fix it and I say, "Okay, honey, I'll get it," and then I get the ladder, climb up and remove the glass cover, unscrew the old bulb, screw in the new bulb, replace the glass cover—done. She tells me the problem, and without even asking me, I know I'm expected to fix it and am happy to do so. And when I do fix it, I receive the spoken or implied response, "Thank you, honey, I appreciate that."

"Don't try to fix it!"

But if you're the expected and designated fixer in the relationship, you find out it can be quite a different story when your partner says something like, "I really had a rough time at work today. There's a lot of work to be done and there's only one of me to do it. I'm really feeling the pressure," and you naturally then slide into fix-it mode. You quickly cycle what they said in your mind and think this:

1) They're talking about a "problem"
2) I'm a trained fixer
3) They wouldn't be telling me about the problem if they didn't expect me to help fix it

4) I'll offer my fix-it solution and

5) They'll implement the solution, solve the problem, be grateful to me for my great advice, and I'll be a hero!

In my case, having quickly cycled that scenario through my brain, I would likely say to my wife, "This is what I think you should do..." And before I'm finished, she says, "Why do you always try to fix things when I'm talking to you? Why can't you just listen?" Whoa, I stop in my tracks. But wait a minute, I don't understand, when she told me about fixing things around the house, those were problems I was expected to fix. Telling me those problems was instruction enough that I was being asked to get them fixed. But telling me this *other* kind of problem was apparently *not* a fix-it situation.

Here's what I'll often tell my class: "Some people are trained fixers. You tell them a problem, and they think you're doing so because you want them to help you fix it. If you want them to just listen to you, then tell them so. Say something like, 'I'm having a problem at work and I want to tell you about it, but I'm not asking you to fix it, I just want you to listen.'" Then the fixer is off the hook— they are not expected to be in fix-it mode but in listen-mode only. And if you're the fixer, to your surprise you may find that your listening itself actually helped *them* fix their own problem because you enabled them to vocalize their problem, hear themselves speak, get a clearer understanding of their issue, and come to their own conclusions as to what needed to be done. In other words, you provided a sounding board for them to work out their own solution.

<u>When</u> to use *Empathic Listening Skill*:

1) The topic is very meaningful or significant to you or the speaker, and/or
2) Emotions are running high, and/or
3) Either of you don't feel understood, and/or
4) Trust is low in your relationship.

These are all cases where we want to intentionally and empathically listen to really understand what the other person is saying and meaning so that there's no misunderstanding each other.

Especially, you will want to use *Empathic Listening Skill* when trust is low in the relationship—when you have some doubts and friction between you. For example, if either or both of you have said hurtful things to each other or have given the cold shoulder to each other. In those cases, it's easy to misunderstand or prejudge what the other person is saying or implying, which would then make matters worse.

Empathic Listening—especially saying back the essence of what you heard the other person say—will slow down the conversation, help avoid misunderstandings, and get you closer to understanding each other correctly. Such listening can help rebuild openness and trust and ultimately help in arriving at resolutions and possibly reviving the relationship if it's been down.

Summary:

The 5 Steps of Empathic Listening Skill:

1) **Quiet your mind and focus on the other person as they are speaking.**
2) **Listen fully and openly to what they are saying.**
3) **Listen "through the words"** to the deeper thoughts and feelings that you sense from the speaker.
4) **Don't interrupt them when they're speaking to you.**
5) **Say back to them, in your own words, what they said and their feelings that you sensed from them** to make sure you understand them correctly and they feel understood.

Self-Reflection:

1) As I reflect on the above, how would I rate my *Empathic Listening Skill* in relation to *(√ below)*:

	Low 1	2	3	4	High 5
People close to me (family, friends, etc.)					.
People at work (co-workers, customers, etc.)					
People in general					

continued next page...

2) Is *Empathic Listening Skill* something I want/need to be more conscious of and better at?

    Yes ___   No ___   Somewhat ___   Not Sure ___

3) If yes or somewhat, what aspects of my listening style would I like to correct or improve?

_____

_____

_____

_____

_____

_____

_____

_____

_____

4) What **actions** will I take to correct or improve my *Empathic Listening Skill*, and with whom?

_____

_____

_____

_____

_____

_____

_____

_____

_____

Let's now look at some of the things we may be doing that block good listening...

Chapter Six

Listening Blocks to Effective Communication

*Things that get in the way of listening well,
and we may not even realize we're doing them.*

There are many blocks that can interfere with listening effectively, and we need to be aware of them in our communication with others. Here are some of the most common ones:

- **Mind Reading** – Thinking you already know what they are thinking and saying without really listening to them. Such as thinking, *I've heard all this before—same old stuff.* Mind reading prevents you from having an open mind to hear what the person is saying now.

- **Rehearsing** – Thinking of how you will respond instead of being fully present and hearing what they are saying now. Such as, *I know exactly what I'm going to tell her when her lips stop moving.* Rehearsing means you're listening to your own thoughts instead of theirs.

- **Filtering** – Selective Listening – Hearing only what you want to hear instead of what they're actually saying. Such as thinking, *I like these points they're saying (while I'm ignoring the ones I don't like).* Filtering blocks out things that may be uncomfortable for you to hear, but the speaker *wants* you to hear and understand.

- **Daydreaming** – Thinking of other things while someone is talking to you. *Spacing out! "Hmm, I wonder where I'll go for dinner tonight?"* Not being present and totally missing what is being said.
- **Advising** – Jumping in with your unsolicited suggestions or solutions to their problem when all they want you to do is listen. *"I don't think you're doing it right; what I'd do in that situation is…"* Advising, though well-intended, can actually take over the conversation when the speaker simply wants to be heard and have their feelings empathized with.
- **Judging** – Analyzing, critiquing, and contesting what the speaker is saying, rather than simply listening to try to understand their point of view. Thinking, *"No, you've got it wrong, that's not how I see it!"*
- **Condescending** – The One Upper – Overriding what the other person is saying. *"That's nothing… Wait till you hear what happened to ME!"* Condescending can make the other person feel that what they had to say wasn't important and that your story was better than theirs. This can feel like a putdown to the speaker.

Self-Reflection:

Which of these Listening Blocks do I do? *(√ below):*

	Often	Some-times	Rarely	Not at All
Mind Reading				
Rehearsing				
Filtering				
Daydreaming				
Advising				
Judging				
Condescending				
Other:				
Other:				

How to Avoid the Listening Blocks:

Each of these listening blocks takes you away from quieting your mind and focusing on what the speaker is saying and feeling in the here and now. **The best way to avoid these blocks is to <u>practice *Empathic Listening Skill*</u>, especially Step 1—*<u>Quiet your mind and focus</u>* on the other person as they are speaking to you.** As you do, these listening blocks will start to disappear and be replaced with good, effective listening.

In these past two chapters, we reviewed do's and don'ts of effective listening to others, now let's look at how we can effectively express ourselves...

Chapter Seven

Key 3: Empathic Speaking Skill

The Question: "How can I say what I want to say in a way that accurately expresses my thoughts and feelings, and at the same time increases the likelihood the other person will be open to hear and receive it, whether it's a pleasant and agreeable topic or something we disagree on, or even something I'm upset about?"

Empathic Speaking Skill has 5 steps:

Step 1: Clarify and organize your thoughts before you speak. *"If you blurt, you could hurt!"*

This is a big one. How many times have you blurted out some hurtful words when you were really upset only to feel within seconds that it was an insensitive, damaging thing to do? In my classes, I'll ask that same question, "How many of you have blurted out some angry words in the heat of the moment, totally blasting the other person, only to feel bad about it soon after?" Nearly everyone raises their hand. It may have been a cathartic, emotional release in the moment, but the fallout was usually negative. If we can just hit the "pause" button for a second, gather ourselves, recognize our feelings, and more thoughtfully choose the words and tone of voice that expresses our concerns, then we will be much more likely to have our concerns heard and received by the other person—which is our goal anyway.

If you blurt out angry, hurtful words with a harsh tone of voice, the listener will likely do one of three things, often referred to as the <u>Fight, Flight or Freeze Response</u>:

1) <u>Fight:</u> Lash back at you with the same kind of angry language, in which case the argument escalates and can even spin out of control; or

2) <u>Flight (Flee):</u> Get very defensive, withdraw and shut down, and throw up a wall of silence because they don't want to get stung or make matters worse; or

3) <u>Freeze:</u> Be stunned, shocked, and unsure how to feel or react. Basically, frozen in place like a deer caught in the headlights.

None of these scenarios is helpful, and none of them result in what you're hoping for, which is to express your concerns and feelings and receive an understanding, empathic response from the person you're speaking to.

If you simply blow off steam and your words and mannerisms hurt others, especially the people you love and care about, though it may be a cathartic, emotional release for you it can create a lot of immediate and long-term relationship damage. Think before you speak—how it will come out, and how it will be received.

"I-Statements" vs. "You-Statements"

Here's an effective method for expressing your thoughts and feelings in a non-inflammatory way: Prepare to speak in **"I-Statements"**, such as, "I think...", "I feel...", "I want...", "I would like...", "I'm concerned...", etc.

"I-Statements" show that your statements come from *you*—your thoughts, feelings, and concerns—and are much easier for the listener to receive and respond to than finger-pointing, accusatory "You-Statements", which are often expressed and received as flames. The listener will react against those negative expressions because they don't want to get burned.

Examples of "You-Statements" restated as "I-Statements":

- "You're way too loud!" can be restated,
    "I would like you to please lower your voice."

- "You never listen to me!" can be restated,
    "I want you to listen to me when I'm speaking to you."

- "You make me so angry!" can be restated,
    "I feel really upset when you..."

Notice that using "I-Statements" can express your concerns and desires clearly but not in an attacking or accusatory way, thus making it more likely you'll receive less resistance from the listener to what you're saying or requesting than had you expressed yourself with a more aggressive "You-Statement". Of course, you can't control the other person's response, but you can make it a bit easier for them to respond in the ways you're hoping for.

Step 2: Express with <u>respect</u>. Choose your words well, and be aware of your tone of voice. Be sensitive to the heart of the person you're speaking to—if you do, they'll be more likely to listen.

This is a close add-on to Step 1—*how* you say what you want to say. In one of my men's classes in jail, an inmate said, "I don't understand my wife. She wasn't saying much, and I tried to get her to tell me what was wrong and she wouldn't tell me." I asked, "What did you say to her?" He said, "How come you're stomping around the house acting like such a bitch?" The class burst out in laughter, but he was serious. I looked at him and said, "Hmm, I think I see the problem. If you were to put yourself in her shoes, and she said to you, 'How come you're stomping around the house acting like such a jerk?' how would you feel?" "Pretty angry," he said. "Exactly, you'd feel disrespected. That's probably how she felt. Now let's see if we can come up with something she might be open to hear."

We then worked out a better way to say it, something like, "You seem upset. Is there something wrong?" and then I told him to listen to her with an open mind to hear what she had to say. This is an extreme example but illustrative. There's a big difference between, "Why are you acting like such a bitch?" and "What's wrong?"

The reality is that if someone speaks to us disrespectfully, we have no incentive to respond favorably to their concerns or requests and give them the impression that it's okay for them to talk to us like that—even if they're right. Why reward or encourage that kind of mistreatment? If someone speaks to us disrespectfully, we may holler and push back or shut down completely like this inmate's wife did. Again, you reap what you sow. Sow disrespect and it will bounce back at you. Sow respect and there's a greater chance that respect will be returned. We can determine which happens by what comes out of our mouths.

I like this quote by Dr. Frank Luntz: "It's not what you say, it's what people hear." Even if you say the right words, but you say them with a disrespectful tone and attitude, the other person will *hear* the disrespect and *not* your words.

Especially when you're upset it's important to express with respect. Remember, this is a fellow human being you're talking to. Treat them as you would like to be treated.

Step 3: Express your points clearly, what you want or need, what you feel. Don't be vague. Don't expect the other person to read your mind. Speak about one issue at a time.

If you're married or in a committed relationship, you may have said or heard this one before: "If you loved me, you'd know what I want." The problem is this—if we make guessing what we want a requirement of whether a person loves us or not, then they may not guess correctly. It doesn't mean they don't love or care for us, because they do; it simply means they can't tell everything that's going on inside of us. Better that we spell it out—make it clear.

For example, if you want to go out on a dinner date with your spouse or partner, instead of waiting for them to somehow intuit your desire, it's better to spell it out, say what you want. "I'd like to go out on a date together. Can we go out to dinner tonight?" Your message is clear.

The vaguer you are with what you want or need, or what you feel, the more likely the listener will not respond in the ways you would like. It helps them to help you if you express your points to them clearly.

Also, speak about one issue or concern at a time. Don't jump from one thing to another or you may confuse and overwhelm the listener. And be careful not to speak too long on any given point or you might lose the listener's attention. Your goal is to be heard and understood by the listener. Make it easy for them to do so.

Step 4: Pause for the listener's response. If they don't say anything after you've spoken, you might ask, "What did you understand about what I said?" or "I'm interested to know what you think and feel about what I said." Then listen to their response.

Again, the more important, serious or emotion-filled the topic the more it's vital that you communicate clearly and then give the other person a chance to respond. Ideally, they will know how to do *Empathic Listening* and say back in their own words the main points they heard you say and the feelings they sensed in you, and then afterward express their own thoughts and feelings on the subject. But even if they don't know these communication skills, you can invite them to respond.

Either way, pausing for their response lets them know you are interested in knowing what they heard, if they have any questions or what they feel about the subject. This helps avoid any misunderstandings between the two of you now or later regarding this important matter.

Step 5: Thank them for listening to you. You can simply say, *"Thanks for listening."*

If the person has heard you out, and invested their time and energy to do so, it's important to appreciate them for it. A simple *"Thank you"* lets them know their listening was important to you, affirms them for it, and encourages them to continue to be good listeners in the future. Don't take their listening for granted—thank them for it. They'll appreciate being appreciated.

Summary:

The 5 Steps of Empathic Speaking Skill:
1) **Clarify** and **organize** your thoughts **before** you speak.
2) **Express with respect.** Be sensitive to the heart of the person you're speaking to.
3) **Express your points clearly.**
4) **Pause for the listener's response.**
5) **Thank them for listening to you.**

Self-Reflection:
1) As I reflect on the above, how would I rate my *Empathic Speaking Skill* in relation to *(√ below)*:

	Low				High
	1	2	3	4	5
People close to me (family, friends, etc.)					
People at work (co-workers, customers, etc.)					
People in general					

2) Is *Empathic Speaking Skill* something I want/need to be more conscious of and better at?

    Yes ___   No ___   Somewhat ___   Not Sure ___

continued next page...

3) If yes or somewhat, what aspects of my speaking style would I like to correct or improve?

_____

_____

_____

_____

_____

_____

_____

_____

_____

4) What **actions** will I take to correct or improve my *Empathic Speaking Skill*, and with whom?

_____

_____

_____

_____

_____

_____

_____

_____

_____

But how about when I'm angry or upset...

Chapter Eight

Expressing Yourself When You're Upset

We all experience moments when someone does or says something that upsets us. When that happens, it's easy to get angry and frustrated and react by saying or doing something that we'll probably regret or we close down, bury our feelings, and feel resentful about it. Either way, those are negative reactions that produce negative consequences.

An alternative is to **pause**, take a breath, and express your feelings without accusing and inflammatory language, tone of voice or demeanor.

An **XYZ Statement** is an excellent method for expressing how you feel and what you want, with the use of the "I-Statement" discussed earlier. Here's how it flows:

XYZ Statement Format:
Fill in the blanks (or on a sheet of paper write):

X – *"When you (name their words or actions) ...*

_____

Y – *(its effect on you) ...*

_____

Z – *"I felt (name your feelings about it) ...*

_____

Examples of an XYZ Statement:

Example 1:

XYZ: "When you yelled at me when we were discussing our finances this morning (X), I was stunned (Y), and I felt very misunderstood and hurt by that (Z)."

Result: This XYZ message communicates clearly your feelings of being misunderstood and hurt but expressed in a non-attacking way.

Better than saying: "Stop yelling at me, you jerk!"

Example 2:

XYZ: "When you didn't come home when you said you would (X), I thought something bad had happened to you (Y), and I felt really worried (Z)."

Result: This XYZ message expresses your feelings of being worried without berating the person for not calling you.

Better than saying: "You're so inconsiderate! Why didn't you call me to say you'd be late?"

Example 3:

XYZ: "When you were late submitting the report (X), I got behind in my own work (Y), and I'm very upset and angry about that (Z)."

Result: This XYZ message expresses how upset you are and what you want in the future but doesn't demean the person you're speaking to.

Better than saying: "What's wrong with you—can't you get your reports in on time?"

Keep the Problem the Problem

When a problem arises between two people, it's very easy for one person to think the other person *is* the problem. However, if we think that way and make the other person "the problem" then we in effect dehumanize them – i.e., we perceive them no longer as a person, but as a problem that needs to be fixed. No wonder they react against what we want or say in that moment because they don't want to be disrespectfully treated like that (and neither would we).

The better and more accurate way to proceed is to think, *"I have a problem with this person's behavior that I need to talk with them about."* This puts the problem in the third position separate from yourself and the other person. This then enables two human beings who fundamentally respect each other to more mindfully and thoughtfully discuss the issue of concern. By proceeding in this manner, especially using *Empathic Speaking and Listening Skills,* and a tool like the XYZ Statement, the conversation is more likely to be constructive with a positive outcome more possible.

The Problem with Silence

We've all heard the phrase "Silence is golden." While that may be true in some instances, when it comes to effective communication, silence can be a problem.

For example, if you're upset at me about something I said or did but you don't say anything about it, I may not automatically get the message of what's bothering you.

We've seen this in other forms of communication, or miscommunication, such as in emails or phone text messages—you send a message to a person and don't hear anything back and then think, *They didn't respond—did they not get the message, or are they angry about what I communicated? I have no idea.*

Remove all doubt. Try to communicate your feelings and what's on your mind clearly so that the other person knows. Again, an XYZ Statement is an excellent way to do so.

But What if They React and Push Back?

After you've delivered your XYZ Statement pause for the listener's response to what you have said. If they received your XYZ Statement well and agree to modify or correct the behavior that bothered or upset you, then it was a successful communication. However, if they react and push back against your statement, then listen empathically to their response so that you understand them and they feel heard and understood. Then, after empathically listening to them like that, you can restate your XYZ Statement if that is still how you feel. You may need to go back and forth like this several times until you both achieve a level of mutual understanding of how to deal with the issue, and perhaps problem-solve the situation where one or both of you agree to make some behavior modifications to achieve a satisfactory resolution.

Benefits of an XYZ Statement

The key to remember here is that an XYZ Statement enables you to express yourself clearly—your thoughts, feelings, concerns, desires—but in a calm, non-accusatory way that creates a greater possibility of the listener responding in ways you hope they will.

Self-Reflection:

Think of something someone did or said recently that bothered or upset you (your spouse, child, parent, co-worker, etc.). Now, **write your XYZ Statement below** (fill in the blanks):

X – *"When you (name their words or actions) ...*

_____

_____

Y – *(its effect on you) ...*

_____

_____

Z – *"I felt (name your feelings about it) ...*

_____

_____

<u>Action:</u> Then pick the right time and place to express your XYZ Statement to them in a calm, non-accusatory manner. Afterward, evaluate how well it was expressed and received, and what you learned from that experience to be even better at it next time.

Chapter Nine

Key 4: Empathic Dialogue

Communication Skills slow down the conversation to enable understanding to happen faster.

The Skill: Put Empathic Speaking and Empathic Listening together to create Empathic Dialogue, which is going back and forth speaking and listening to each other using the skills.

Communication skills take time and effort to do properly, but their value is that they slow down the communication process to enable mutual understanding of each other to happen more quickly.

You can use *Empathic Speaking and Empathic Listening Skills* to talk through a wide range of topics, whatever the emotion. One person speaks and the other person listens with empathy, and then you switch and the speaker becomes the listener, the listener becomes the speaker, and the conversation goes back and forth in this fashion until you both have communicated what you need to on the topic.

In a heated discussion, if even one person in the relationship understands and uses the skills, it will generally calm down the conversation and have a positive effect on how their dialogue unfolds even if the other person has no knowledge or experience of using the skills.

Also, *Empathic Dialogue* is not simply for discussing problem issues where emotions are running high. It can be used for discussing any topic—happy, sad, upset, curious—whatever. The key is to respectfully listen and speak to each other where each person feels heard and understood.

Below are some sample dialogue topic ideas for couples, for talking with your child, your adult child, and in the workplace. I'm sure you can come up with many more topics in which to use the empathic communication skills we've covered in this book.

Dialogue Topics for Couples		
Time Together	Go on a Date	Child/Children
Parenting Styles	Finances	Budget
Job/Work	Problem/Issue	Hurt/Anger/Fear
Inspirations	Faith/Church	Life Goals
World News	Volunteerism	Health
Recreation/Exercise	Hobbies	Reading/Books
Relatives	Friends	Vacation
Walks in Nature	Dreams/Aspirations	*and more!*

Dialogue Topics with Your Child		
(considering the child's age – i.e., very young up to late teen)		
School	Friends	Hopes/Dreams
Hobbies	Toys	Video Games
Sports	Worries/Fears	Challenges
Favorite Foods	Favorite Book	Favorite Movie
Fun Thing to Do	Favorite Places to Go	*and more!*

Dialogue Topics with Your Adult Child		
School	Job/Work	Hobbies
Friends	Hopes/Dreams	Life Goals
Relationship	Wants/Needs	Worries/Fears
Challenges	Finances	Politics
Social Issues	Environmental Issues	Future Plans
Favorite Foods	Favorite Book	Favorite Movie
Fun Thing to Do	Favorite Places to Go	*and more!*

Dialogue Topics for the Workplace *(with appropriate personnel—i.e., manager, co-worker, etc.)*		
Meeting Agendas	New Project	Reports Due
Getting Assistance	Appreciation	Work Sharing
Team Goals	Problem/Issue	Hurt/Anger/Fear
Inspirations	Innovation	Supplies
Cleanliness	Loud Talking	Workplace Safety
Complaints	Tardiness	Work Overload
Worries	Salary Increase	Frustrations
Work-Life Balance	Future Plans	*and more!*

Talking Through Tough Issues

These communication skills we've covered are especially useful in helping couples and individuals dialogue successfully through difficult, emotionally-laden topics. The skills help keep the conversation safe and on track.

A few years ago, during one of my classes, I asked couples to use the speaking and listening skills they had just learned to dialogue in their twosomes and work through a minor problem they had.

After about 20 minutes, I asked for the class to regather as a group. I then asked how their dialogues went and if any pairs were able to arrive at a resolution to the problem they discussed. After a few responses, one fellow raised his hand and said, "We used the skills and worked through an issue, but the skills take a long time to do— one person speaks, and the other listens and says back what they heard, then we switched roles, and the other person spoke, and the other person listened, and then we repeated that process. I mean it takes a long time to go back and forth like that. I'm not sure that's going to be very realistic to do in real life."

I asked how long they had that problem going on in their relationship, and he said, "Oh, we've been dealing with that thing for about 5 years!" As soon as he said it, he realized that 20 minutes of skilled communication producing a resolution was far more effective and faster than 5 years of frequent non-skilled communication without a resolution.

To this very point, Stephen Covey said, "Empathic listening takes time, but it doesn't take anywhere near as much time as it takes to back up and correct misunderstandings when you're already miles down the road; to redo; to live with unexpressed and unresolved problems; to deal with the results of not giving people psychological air."

In order for the skills to work, it takes time and practice to use them well. Over time, their use gets easier and more of a habit and preferred way to speak and listen. Skills become habits through our practice, and habits eventually become our behavior and the way we will more naturally prefer to communicate. So it's important to practice the skills correctly from the beginning.

Self-Reflection:

Who should I have a conversation with and about what?

Name	Topic	When	Result

Action: Then schedule the time to have these conversations as soon as possible and actually do them.

Helpful Tip: *Put this information in whatever you use to schedule and accomplish your daily activities, such as in your cell phone calendar or day planner, so that the information is clearly seen as a reminder and not out of sight and out of mind.*

Chapter Ten

The 3 A's:
Applaud, Admire, Appreciate

"Appreciation can make a day, even change a life.
Your willingness to put it into words is all that is necessary."
~ Margaret Cousins

Expressing these 3 A's <u>often</u>—with <u>sincerity</u>—is one of the best things you can do to encourage and support the people in your life. They build the bonds of heart and closeness and are another important element of good communication.

For something someone said or did that you were impressed by or grateful for, simply say:
"I *applaud (or congratulate)* you for…"
"I *admire* you for…"
"I *appreciate* you for…"

Say *what* it is you applaud, admire or appreciate the person for. It means you not only applaud, admire or appreciate them in general but for the specific thing they did.

For example:
"I want to *applaud (or congratulate)* you for that great speech you gave last night."

"I really *admire* the way you accomplished that project."

"I *appreciate* you for doing the extra chores."

You might think the person already knows that you applaud, admire or appreciate them, but how are they to know for sure unless you actually tell them? Remove all doubt and let them know.

In my classes, one of my favorite exercises is when I ask participants to face each other as couples or in pairs and ask them to say one thing they appreciate about each other and why. After a few minutes, I call an end to the exercise and ask, "What was it like to be appreciated like that?" and they say it felt great to hear it. "What was it like to express the appreciation?" and they say it felt great to say it.

Then I ask a follow-up question: "How many of you were appreciated by your partner for something you didn't even know they noticed, let alone appreciated you for?" Almost always several hands go up, and their partner—especially if they are a couple—looks at them a bit stunned as if to say, "I thought it was obvious I appreciated you for that." I ask the person who raised their hand why they raised their hand, and they typically reply, "I suspected that he (or she) appreciated me for that, but I wasn't sure. But when I actually heard the words, I knew they did." It's a great lesson for everyone the power and impact of expressed appreciation.

Also, when we get into the habit of verbally expressing applause, admiration, and appreciation to others for things they have said or done for us, it helps us grow into a person of gratitude in the process.

We can also do this in written form in a letter, email, text or otherwise. The main thing is that we express it.

Self-Reflection:

Who are the people in my life I can *Applaud, Admire,* or *Appreciate* and the reasons why?

Name	For Doing/Being

Action: *Bring a smile to someone's face today—let them know what you applaud, admire or appreciate about them, and be specific. They'll appreciate hearing it!*

Chapter Eleven

Nurture Your Relationship Garden

"The master of the garden is the one who waters it, trims the branches, plants the seeds, and pulls the weeds."
~ Vera Nazarian

Let's say you want to make a vegetable garden. You prepare the soil, plant the seeds, and water it. You stand back and look proudly on what you've done. It looks all set to produce the bounty you're hoping for.

But what if you don't pay attention to the garden for a few months and come back thinking, *Ah, I'm ready for those ripe tomatoes now.* What will you find? Probably a lot of dead or dying plants. What else will you discover? The weeds have taken over. What happened to the garden? It was prepared and planted well in the beginning but neglected for far too many days and literally dried up.

A relationship is similar to the garden. Even if it starts off well, if the relationship is not nourished and cared for, it can wane and even perish.

Don't take your relationships for granted, especially the most meaningful ones in your life. Relationships are living things that require care and nutrients to grow well. The care is the love and intentionality we invest into them. The nutrients are the things we actually *do*—the quality time we spend together, the ways we support each other, the words of encouragement—and our communication skills are the means we use to tend the relationship. When we do, the relationship garden will grow strong and healthy through its seasons.

Ways to Tend Your Relationships

Each relationship is its own garden. They are not all the same. Your relationship with your spouse is different from the relationship you have with your child or co-worker and so forth. You need to tend each relationship individually, thoughtfully, doing what each one needs to grow well, especially the ones nearest and dearest to you.

Here's a simple strategy: Sit down with a sheet of paper and make 3 columns (or use the form on the next page). In the first column on the left write down some of their names. In the middle column next to their name jot down what might be a good next step to nurture that specific relationship. In the column on the right, write down when you will do it. Here are some examples:

- A phone call, letter or email just to say hi and catch up on how you're both doing
- An invitation to get together for coffee or lunch, go to a movie, or take a walk around the block
- An encouraging word for a job well done
- Then do it immediately or schedule the day and time to make it happen—without a schedule, and actually following through and doing your plan, it will just be good intentions with no substance and no result
- For example, you can format your to-do list like this:

Name	Next Step	When
Mom	Call to check-in	2-3 times weekly
Jane (spouse)	Plan a date out together	This coming Friday or Sat.?
Michael (child)	Personal time together	This evening after dinner
John (friend)	Meet for lunch	One day this month – 10th or 11th?
Mary (co-worker)	Email to thank her for her help on project	Do now

Action: Schedule when to do those things, then follow through and do them.

The above ideas are simple actions on your part, but they can go a long way in nurturing your relationships on a consistent basis.

Who haven't you spoken with lately? Is it time to give them a call and say hello?

Name	Next Step	When

Helpful Tip: If you get the sudden inspiration to contact someone, seize the moment and do it right then. It may be just what they needed at that time. You can simply say, "I was thinking about you. How are you?" They will be moved.

Chapter Twelve

Practice Makes Permanent

"If you want to get good at anything where real-life performance matters, you actually have to practice that skill in context. Study by itself is never enough."
~ Josh Kaufman

A very common expression is "Practice Makes Perfect" but there's another version that I find more accurate. "Practice Makes Permanent." Why? Because if you practice something incorrectly, the incorrect behavior will become permanent—which is not what you want.

Think of a golfer. If he has been practicing the same bad swing over and over since he started playing the game, he will achieve a perfectly bad swing that is very likely a permanently bad swing unless he gets it corrected.

Likewise, if we have been in the habit of practicing imperfect communication styles for most of our lives, then we will inevitably end up with negative results, i.e., poor communication, unsatisfactory relationships, etc.

But if we learn effective communication skills and practice them *correctly* over and over again, eventually we will get closer to perfecting those skills and making them permanent in our behavior and in our relationships. And when we get off track, or forget to use the skills, we can refresh our understanding of the skills and start practicing them again to get back on track just like that golfer who does an errant swing, refocuses on doing the correct swing motion, and then tries again to do it right.

Habits Become Behavior

The more we practice a skill correctly—and do so consistently over time—the more it becomes a habit and ultimately our behavior. I like this explanation of habit formation from *Psychology Today*: "Habit formation is the process by which new behaviors become automatic...Old habits are hard to break and new habits are hard to form. That's because the behavioral patterns we repeat most often are literally etched into our neural pathways. The good news is that, through repetition, it's possible to form—and maintain—new habits."

Conscious daily practice of the communication skills we've covered in this book is the key for them to become our communication habits and ultimately our default communication behavior. But keep in mind, just like the professional golfer who won the tournament yesterday but is back on the practice tee the following morning, it's important to keep the good practice going to keep honing and improving our skills—and, as a result, grow and strengthen our relationships.

Chapter Thirteen

NOW is the Time!

If not now, when; if not me, who?

We only have the present. The past is past, and the future isn't here yet. We live in the here and now. Change is only possible in the here and now.

All the skills we've learned only have value in their implementation—step by step. We know this is true with learning "hard skills"—like driving a car, playing the guitar or typing on a keyboard. These are physical activities that take intentional, focused, physical practice to become proficient at. But the same is also true for "soft skills", which can be defined as "personal attributes that enable someone to interact effectively and harmoniously with other people" (from google.com). Communication skills are soft skills in that they develop attributes to interact well with others.

Knowledge is simply information in our heads, but what we *do* with that knowledge in our *actions* will determine whether or not we actually grew and benefited from that knowledge.

By now you may have realized that this is really a self-improvement book—that your relationships will grow and improve to the extent that you do. Many times in my classes people will say that when they were walking into the room as a couple, they hoped their partner

---

would learn something from the class only to discover that it was they themselves who needed to learn and improve.

I hope you gained some meaningful information from the previous pages. I have found that these skills work in my own life and have benefited the lives and relationships of so many others, and I hope you incorporate them into your life as well. Review the skill steps and put them into practice a little bit each day—at home, at work, everywhere.

The point is to make changes, even if they're small, because regardless of the magnitude of the change you will be better off than when you started. The following pages offer a way to get started—and make progress one day at a time.

Action Guide

Take the...
12-Day Communication Challenge!
Improving Your Skills One Day At A Time!!

Starting today or tomorrow, or a day very soon, begin your 12-day journey to put the empathic communication skills we've covered in this book into practice in your life right away.

The **Goal** is to steadily improve your Empathic Awareness, Listening, Speaking and Dialogue Skills to become a more effective communicator in building strong relationships with the important people in your life.

Get Better Each Day

Now, to be clear, you won't magically become perfect in using these skills in 12 days. Behavior modification doesn't occur that quickly. Building new habits takes deliberate, consistent practice. But you can make meaningful strides as you consciously put these skills into practice, in the moment, one day at a time. As James Clear writes in his article *How Long Does It Actually Take to Form a New Habit? (Backed by Science)*: "At the end of the day, how long it takes to form a particular habit doesn't really matter that much. Whether it takes 50 days or 500 days, you have to put in the work either way... The only way to get to Day 500 is to start with Day 1. So, forget about the number and focus on doing the work."

Or, as the Nike commercial says, *"Just do it!"*

Here's How It Works

What follows are 12 pages, one for each day, with one or two skill steps per day. Simply <u>read aloud to yourself the specific page</u> in the morning and often during that particular day and consciously focus on practicing that skill step or steps with the people you communicate with throughout that day, and do the same for each day—that's it!

It's best if you can memorize and recite from memory the <u>bolded sentence</u> on that page throughout that day—that will help instill those specific skill points in your mind and actions.

<u>Helpful Tips:</u>
1. <u>Keep the skill step(s) of each day handy and visible</u> to you throughout that day.
2. Have a <u>small sticky note</u> on your computer screen that says "<u>Skill Practice</u>".
3. You can set the <u>alarm on your cell phone</u> for certain times during the day to remind you to review the skill step(s) for that day.

These kinds of reminders are important in building new habits, especially in the course of a busy day.

At the end of the day, sit down and do an honest self-evaluation of how well, or not, you used those skills effectively during the day and what you might have done better. Review the individual people and interactions in your mind. Pat yourself on the back if you did a good job; give yourself encouraging words if you didn't. <u>Even a small improvement is a step forward.</u>

Then repeat this format for the next day's instructions, and on and on for the full 12 days. Consistency will be important—don't' skip a day. **Do all 12 days.**

Be patient with yourself. You will probably start Day 1 full of enthusiasm and within a short time realize you had forgotten to practice the skill. Don't be discouraged. That's normal in trying to learn a new skill, make a new habit.

Keep at It! <u>When you realize you haven't been practicing the skill, simply pause, review the skill step for that day, and start practicing it one interaction at a time.</u> You'll have to do this often over the course of each day of the challenge. Again, you're shaping your thinking and awareness of incorporating these skills into your daily life. This is very likely brand new for you. But stay with it. You'll get better at it day by day.

IMPORTANT: Have a fresh and open mind during this 12-Day Challenge, *especially* with the familiar people in your life. Otherwise, it will be easy for you to slide into your normal communication style with those people— with your spouse or partner, your child(ren), co-workers—people you see and interact with all the time. Be different this time! Be pro-active and think, *These are important people in my life. I care about them and my relationship with them. I won't be the same old person communicating in the same old way. Instead, I will practice these skills with a fresh and open mind with each of them.* Make that commitment to yourself then do it! And if any of them ask you why you're behaving differently tell them, "I'm learning and practicing new communication skills. I'm trying to improve how I interact with you and others. I want to be better at it." Trust me, they will probably be impressed that you're making the effort to do so.

Think:
"One day at a time, I will make these skills mine."

Have a Great 12 Days!

Day 1
Empathic Awareness Skill, Steps 1 & 2

"Today is a new day and a new start for me. I will practice Empathic Awareness Skill throughout this day! I commit to becoming a more *Empathic Person.*

I will recognize the <u>inherent value and dignity</u> of myself and each person I meet and communicate with today—how unique and special they are—their unique traits, talents, qualities, abilities.

It will take my focus and determination, but I can do it. I will see myself and others with fresh eyes and heart today and appreciate who I am and who they are as unique human beings!"

+++++

<u>End of Day Reflection:</u> How was my practice of this skill today? What worked well and with whom? Where did I fall short? What can I do better next time?

_____

_____

_____

_____

_____

_____

_____

_____

_____

_____

Day 2
Empathic Awareness Skill, Step 3

"Today, I will <u>desire</u> in my mind to <u>want</u> to listen to the other person as they are speaking to me.

They deserve that respect.

I really want to listen to and understand what they are saying, meaning and feeling in their words and body language.

Today I will make the effort to sincerely Want to listen to each person I interact with. This is my focus for today!"

+++++

End of Day Reflection: How was my practice of this skill today? What worked well and with whom? Where did I fall short? What can I do better next time?

_____

_____

_____

_____

_____

_____

_____

_____

_____

_____

_____

Day 3
Empathic Awareness Skill, Step 4

"Today I will think of the <u>positives</u> in my relationship with each person I communicate with, whether I know them well or not.

I will think about why they are special to me, what unique qualities they have.

I will Shut Out any Negatives I perceive or feel about them. Instead I will Focus on the Positives I see in them.

I will have this Empathic Heart and Mindset with each person I interact with today!"

+++++

End of Day Reflection: How was my practice of this skill today? What worked well and with whom? Where did I fall short? What can I do better next time?

_____

_____

_____

_____

_____

_____

_____

_____

_____

_____

_____

_____

_____

Day 4
Empathic Listening Skill, Step 1

"Today I will transform my listening. I will quiet my mind when others are speaking to me.

I will block out all other thoughts, concerns, and distractions I may have and focus solely on the other person—what they are saying and feeling, what they are trying to communicate to me in that moment. I want to understand them.

Today, I will quiet my mind when I'm listening to others and focus on them."

+++++

End of Day Reflection: How was my practice of this skill today? What worked well and with whom? Where did I fall short? What can I do better next time?

_____

_____

_____

_____

_____

_____

_____

_____

_____

_____

_____

_____

Day 5
Empathic Listening Skill, Steps 2 & 3

"Today I will <u>listen fully and openly</u> when others are speaking to me.

I will put aside my words, or any defensiveness or reaction I may have, and actively listen to them.

I will ask myself, *What are they saying and feeling? What are their needs, wants, concerns, interests, etc.? What are they trying to communicate to me?*, and listen intently.

<u>I will listen through their words</u> to their deeper thoughts and feelings beneath those words. I will focus on doing this with each person I interact with today!"

+++++

<u>End of Day Reflection:</u> How was my practice of this skill today? What worked well and with whom? Where did I fall short? What can I do better next time?

_____

_____

_____

_____

_____

_____

_____

_____

_____

_____

_____

_____

Day 6
Empathic Listening Skill, Step 4

"Today I <u>won't interrupt</u> **people when they are speaking to me.** I'll simply listen and let them finish their sentences.

I won't butt in, or be quick to judge, advise or correct—I will hold my tongue while they are speaking!

I will simply listen to them and try to understand what they are saying and feeling from <u>their</u> point of view. This will take my self-discipline and determined effort. This will be my focus for today!"

+++++

End of Day Reflection: How was my practice of this skill today? What worked well and with whom? Where did I fall short? What can I do better next time?

_____

_____

_____

_____

_____

_____

_____

_____

_____

_____

_____

_____

Day 7
Empathic Listening Skill, Step 5

"Today, in my conversations with others, I will <u>say back to them</u>, in my own words, what they said to me, particularly on any emotional or important topics that come up.

I will simply say back the essence or key points of what they were saying and feeling to make sure I understood them correctly, and so that they feel understood by me.

I will do this with sincerity and focus throughout the day!"

+++++

End of Day Reflection: How was my practice of this skill today? What worked well and with whom? Where did I fall short? What can I do better next time?

_____

_____

_____

_____

_____

_____

_____

_____

_____

_____

_____

_____

Day 8
Empathic Speaking Skill, Step 1

"Today I will <u>clarify and organize</u> my thoughts <u>before</u> I speak.

I won't just blurt out what's on my mind, especially on any emotional topics, or where there's a disagreement.

I will pause and think it through and try to come up with the words, perhaps an XYZ Statement, that will best express what's on my mind and heart, but deliver those words in a respectful, non-accusatory manner and tone of voice.

I want to express myself in such a way that the listener will be open to hear and receive it, whether they agree with me or not. This will be my focus throughout today!"

+++++

End of Day Reflection: How was my practice of this skill today? What worked well and with whom? Where did I fall short? What can I do better next time?

_____

_____

_____

_____

_____

_____

_____

_____

_____

Day 9
Empathic Speaking Skill, Step 2

"Today I will **express with respect.** I will **choose my words well and be aware of my tone of voice. I will be sensitive to the heart of the person I am speaking to.**

I will focus on them, their feelings, their receptivity.

Whatever the topic—whether a pleasant one or not—I will be honest and straightforward, but I will speak to them respectfully and with care.

I will have this heart and attitude today!"

+++++

End of Day Reflection: How was my practice of this skill today? What worked well and with whom? Where did I fall short? What can I do better next time?

_____

_____

_____

_____

_____

_____

_____

_____

_____

_____

_____

_____

_____

Day 10
Empathic Speaking Skill, Step 3

"Today I will <u>express my points clearly</u> when I speak to people—what I want or need, what's on my mind, what I feel.

I won't be vague or ambiguous leaving the listener to guess and wonder what I mean or what I want.

I will think things through and express my points clearly so that others can understand me. I will do this throughout today!"

+++++

End of Day Reflection: How was my practice of this skill today? What worked well and with whom? Where did I fall short? What can I do better next time?

_____

_____

_____

_____

_____

_____

_____

_____

_____

_____

_____

_____

Day 11
Empathic Speaking Skill, Step 4

"Today I will <u>thank people</u> who listen to me, particularly on any important or heartfelt topics. I will simply say, 'Thanks for listening.' I will say it verbally where possible, but at the very least I will say it internally in my own mind.

I will sincerely appreciate them for listening to what I had to say and the feelings I conveyed.

Today, I will say 'Thanks for listening' to the people who listen to me."

+++++

End of Day Reflection: How was my practice of this skill today? What worked well and with whom? Where did I fall short? What can I do better next time?

_____

_____

_____

_____

_____

_____

_____

_____

_____

_____

_____

_____

_____

Day 12
Empathic Dialogue Skill

"Today is a new day! <u>I will review each day's instruction of this challenge and do my best to be aware of and practice each step of the Empathic Awareness, Listening and Speaking Skills</u> that I learned and practiced these past several days!

Today, when people speak to me, I will listen with empathy and respect.

When I speak to people, I will do so with empathy and respect.

I will try to be aware of and practice <u>*all*</u> of these skills today!"

+++++

End of Day Reflection: How was my practice of this skill today? What worked well and with whom? Where did I fall short? What can I do better next time?

I did it! I completed the 12-Day Challenge!

_____

_____

_____

_____

_____

_____

_____

_____

_____

_____

Congratulations!

You completed the
12-Day Communication Challenge!

That's a big accomplishment! I hope you learned a lot from this experience and your communication skills improved. Now continue what you started.

Becoming a skilled communicator is a lifelong journey. The key is Learning and Understanding what to do, coupled with Commitment and Practice of actually doing it and getting better at it one day at a time.

Repeat this 12-Day Communication Challenge in the future. You can also change it up and practice just one of the skills, such as Empathic Listening, for several days in a row to try to get stronger in using that particular skill. The point is to mindfully and steadily develop and grow your communication skills on a daily basis. As you do, your Empathy and ability to Listen, Speak and Dialogue well with others will continue to grow and improve!

If you had a positive experience reading this book and doing the challenge, please tell your friends and suggest they buy and read the book and try the challenge themselves.

I Wish You the Very Best in Using These Skills to Make Great Relationships with the Important People in Your Life!

Acknowledgements

I would not have written this book if I hadn't learned and experienced so much in the field of interpersonal communication from some very special people.

Thanks to Dr. Bernard G. Guerney Jr., and Mary Ortwein who co-authored Mastering the Mysteries of Love™ and Ready for Love™, excellent relationship skills curricula for couples and singles respectively. These programs are born out of Dr. Guerney's Relationship Enhancement™ curriculum, and the communication skills they teach have transformed so many lives, including my own, particularly their insights into the power of listening to truly understand. I also appreciated Mary's wise and caring tutoring of me along the way to become a program facilitator and ultimately a trainer of facilitators of these programs.

Thanks to Dr. Carolyn Curtis who taught the Relationship Enhancement class in Sacramento where my journey in this field began in April 2005, and thanks also to Dennis Stoica who co-taught with Mary the very first facilitator training of Mastering the Mysteries of Love, which my wife and I attended in Oakland in June 2005.

Thanks to Patty Howell and Ralph Jones, my dear friends and work colleagues and co-authors of World Class Marriage™ and World Class Relationships for Work & Home™. They trained me as an instructor in these fine courses that I have taught to many hundreds of couples and individuals. Patty and Ralph model the love and pillars they speak of in their own lives and marriage, and it's a beauty to behold and try to emulate.

Special love and thanks to my wonderfully supportive wife Kimiko—who lovingly tries to keep me on track with these skills on a daily basis to be a better person and husband—and to my son Yong-Sung and daughters Yu-Mee and Jin-Mee who are teaching me with their love and patience how to be a better father every day.

Particular thanks to Jin-Mee for her many hours professionally editing this book, and to a few dear friends who read my drafts and gave me their excellent suggestions. You all helped me so much!

Lastly, thanks to all the couples and individuals I've had the pleasure of teaching these courses to over the past several years. You are an inspiration to me. I learned so much from you and hope you learned as much from me.

Thank you all for being part of this great journey of creating healthy, thriving relationships.

~ Bento

About the Author

Bento has worked full time as a communication and relationship skills instructor with a non-sectarian, non-profit organization in California since 2007. He has taught thousands of couples and singles in classroom-type settings in various venues throughout the state and primarily where he lives in the San Francisco-Oakland Bay Area. In addition, he has developed his own communication skills workshop, titled "Enrich Your Relationships", where he teaches the skills covered in this book.

"I'm always excited when I see people make breakthroughs in their communication skills and relationships," he says. "That fuels my passion and gives me the power and energy to keep doing this important work. I wish every person success in learning and practicing these powerful skills."

Email: bento@bentoleal.com
Website: www.bentoleal.com

SPECIAL REQUEST!

Thank you again for reading my book!
I hope it was beneficial for you.

I would really appreciate your feedback.

If you haven't done so already,
please go to my book at Amazon,
scroll down the page, and click on
"Write a customer review"
letting me know what you thought of the book
and what you may have gained from it.
I read each review. They help me a lot.

Thanks so much, and all the best to you
and your relationships!
~ Bento

Printed in Great Britain
by Amazon

35301002R10063